Facts About the Buzzard

By Lisa Strattin

© 2022 Lisa Strattin

FREE BOOK

FREE FOR ALL SUBSCRIBERS

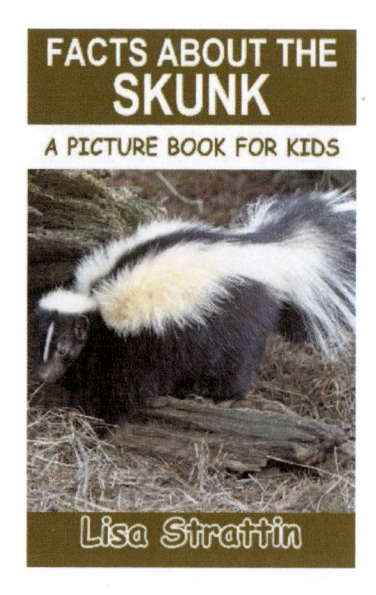

FACTS ABOUT THE SKUNK
A PICTURE BOOK FOR KIDS
Lisa Strattin

LisaStrattin.com/Subscribe-Here

BOX SET

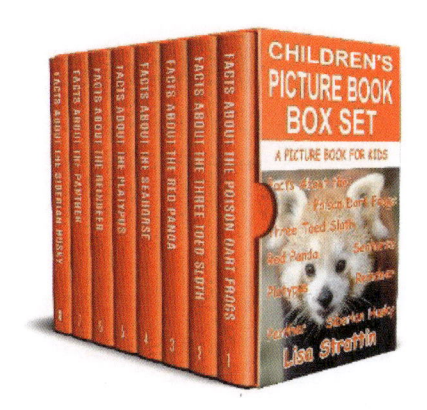

- **FACTS ABOUT THE POISON DART FROGS**
- **FACTS ABOUT THE THREE TOED SLOTH**
  - **FACTS ABOUT THE RED PANDA**
  - **FACTS ABOUT THE SEAHORSE**
  - **FACTS ABOUT THE PLATYPUS**
  - **FACTS ABOUT THE REINDEER**
  - **FACTS ABOUT THE PANTHER**
- **FACTS ABOUT THE SIBERIAN HUSKY**

LisaStrattin.com/BookBundle

Facts for Kids Picture Books by Lisa Strattin

Little Blue Penguin, Vol 92

Chipmunk, Vol 5

Frilled Lizard, Vol 39

Blue and Gold Macaw, Vol 13

Poison Dart Frogs, Vol 50

Blue Tarantula, Vol 115

African Elephants, Vol 8

Amur Leopard, Vol 89

Sabre Tooth Tiger, Vol 167

Baboon, Vol 174

Sign Up for New Release Emails Here

LisaStrattin.com/subscribe-here

All rights reserved. No part of this book may be reproduced by any means whatsoever without the written permission from the author, except brief portions quoted for purpose of review.

All information in this book has been carefully researched and checked for factual accuracy. However, the author and publisher makes no warranty, express or implied, that the information contained herein is appropriate for every individual, situation or purpose and assume no responsibility for errors or omissions. The reader assumes the risk and full responsibility for all actions, and the author will not be held responsible for any loss or damage, whether consequential, incidental, special or otherwise, that may result from the information presented in this book.

All images are free for use or purchased from stock photo sites or royalty free for commercial use.

Some coloring pages might be of the general species due to lack of available images.

I have relied on my own observations as well as many different sources for this book and I have done my best to check facts and give credit where it is due. In the event that any material is used without proper permission, please contact me so that the oversight can be corrected.

COVER IMAGE

https://www.flickr.com/photos/kkoshy/49830003781/

ADDITIONAL IMAGES

https://www.flickr.com/photos/nestorix/44499172265/

https://www.flickr.com/photos/irio/51977704282/

https://www.flickr.com/photos/24874528@N04/50528766917/

https://www.flickr.com/photos/24874528@N04/26126620781/

https://www.flickr.com/photos/128941223@N02/45276266784/

https://www.flickr.com/photos/mountjoy/5194843832/

https://www.flickr.com/photos/nestorix/44499169925/

https://www.flickr.com/photos/andymorffew/51344565295/

https://www.flickr.com/photos/24874528@N04/51328910354/

https://www.flickr.com/photos/15016964@N02/48761049263/

Contents

INTRODUCTION 9

CHARACTERISTICS 11

APPEARANCE 13

LIFE STAGES 15

LIFE SPAN 17

SIZE 19

HABITAT 21

DIET 23

ENEMIES 25

SUITABILITY AS PETS 27

INTRODUCTION

Buzzards, sometimes known as Common Buzzards, are medium-sized birds. This bird's scientific name is *Buteo Buteo*. This bird is also known as the tourist eagle because it is sometimes mistaken for an eagle by European tourists.

Although they are not related to the Common Hawk and belong to a separate family, they are sometimes referred to as hawks in the United States. In Europe and Asia, buzzards are simply known as buzzards, and the Rufous Morph is the most common form of Steppe Buzzard found in the United States.

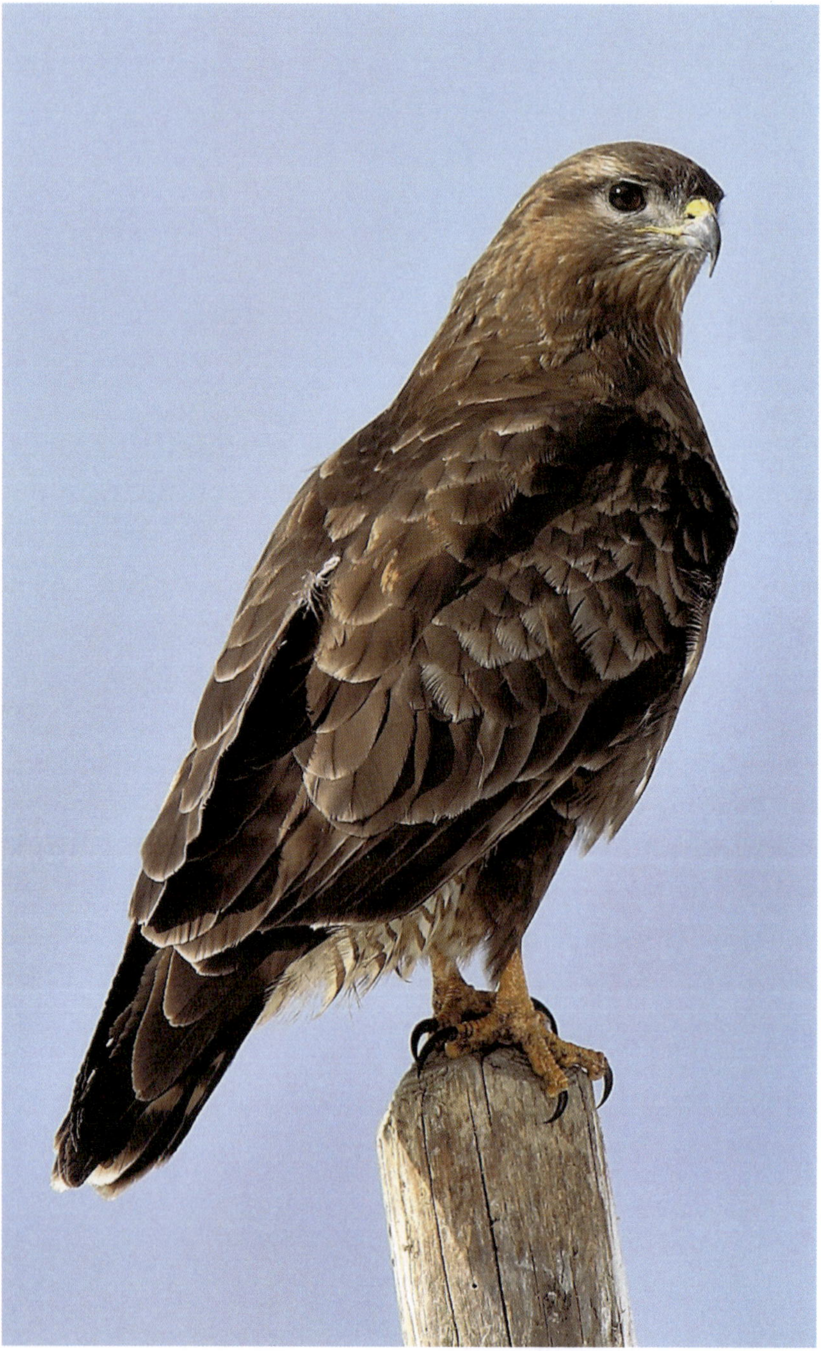

CHARACTERISTICS

The Common Buzzard is a raptor that prefers to hunt on its own. These birds like to be alone in their nests and live with only their mate. They form a team to protect their areas and have a deep bond with their partner.

To warn its companion of any threats, the buzzard communicates or calls with a hiss or a screech. They have also been observed spotting their prey from afar and flying straight towards it. They come to a halt and hover about their target for a few moments before crashing down on them. This permits them to kill their prey with pinpoint accuracy.

Individual buzzards in different localities have varied migratory tendencies. The weather conditions where they live cause some to migrate further south than others. Some buzzards just travel a short distance to reach a warmer climate with more prey to eat during the winter.

The Steppe Buzzard is one of the species that migrates particularly far in the winter. Steppe Buzzards migrate from Asia Minor to the Cape of Africa beginning in September and October. In March, they return to their nesting habitats for the second time.

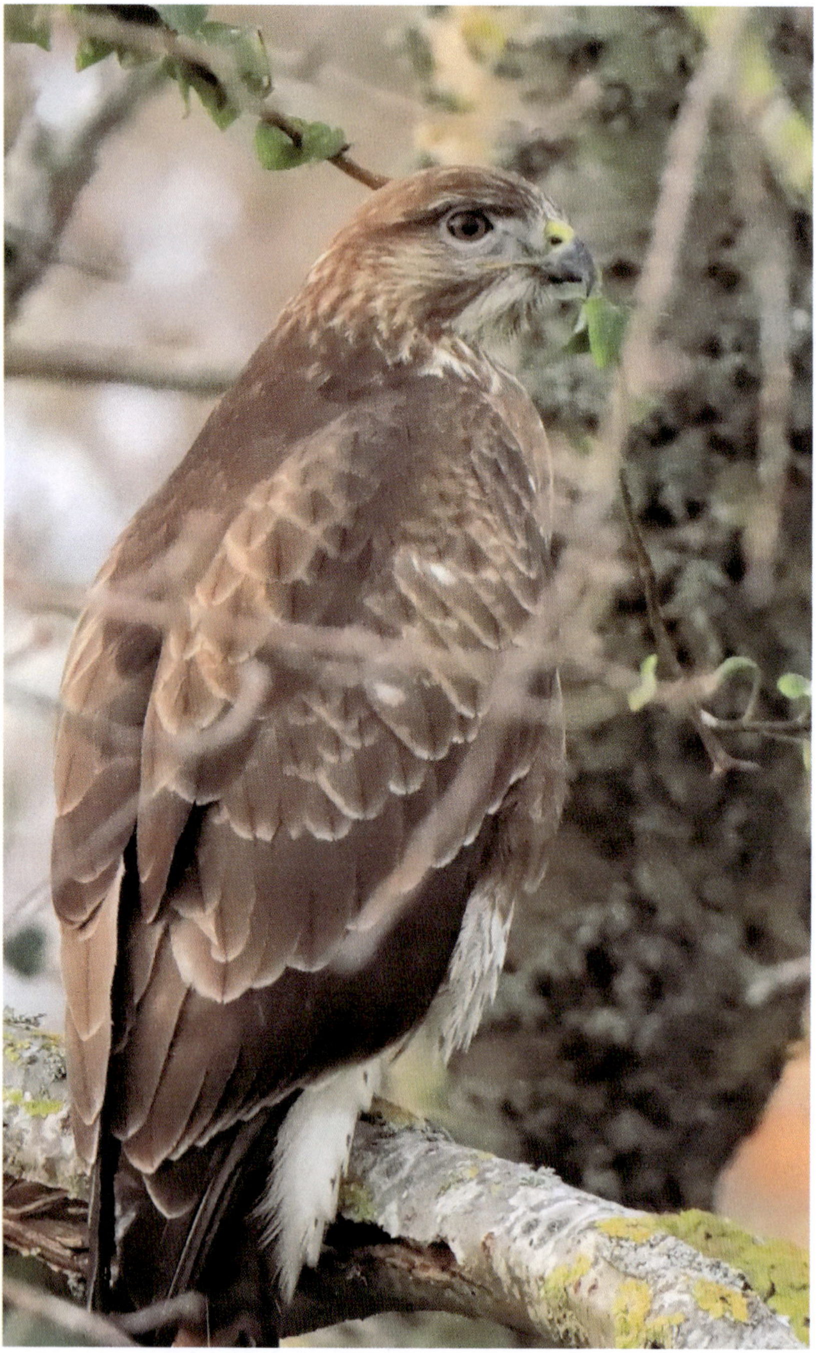

APPEARANCE

Buzzards are medium-sized birds with brown and white markings on their bodies. Their feathers darken near the tips, revealing gray and black colors. Their eyes, with a piercing black in the center and a clear yellow border around the sides, give them a ferocious appearance.

Their bright yellow claws stand out from afar, and their beak hues range from black to yellow, matching their body color. With black on the borders, a band of white, and then dark brown as you go closer to the body, their huge wingspan becomes the focal point.

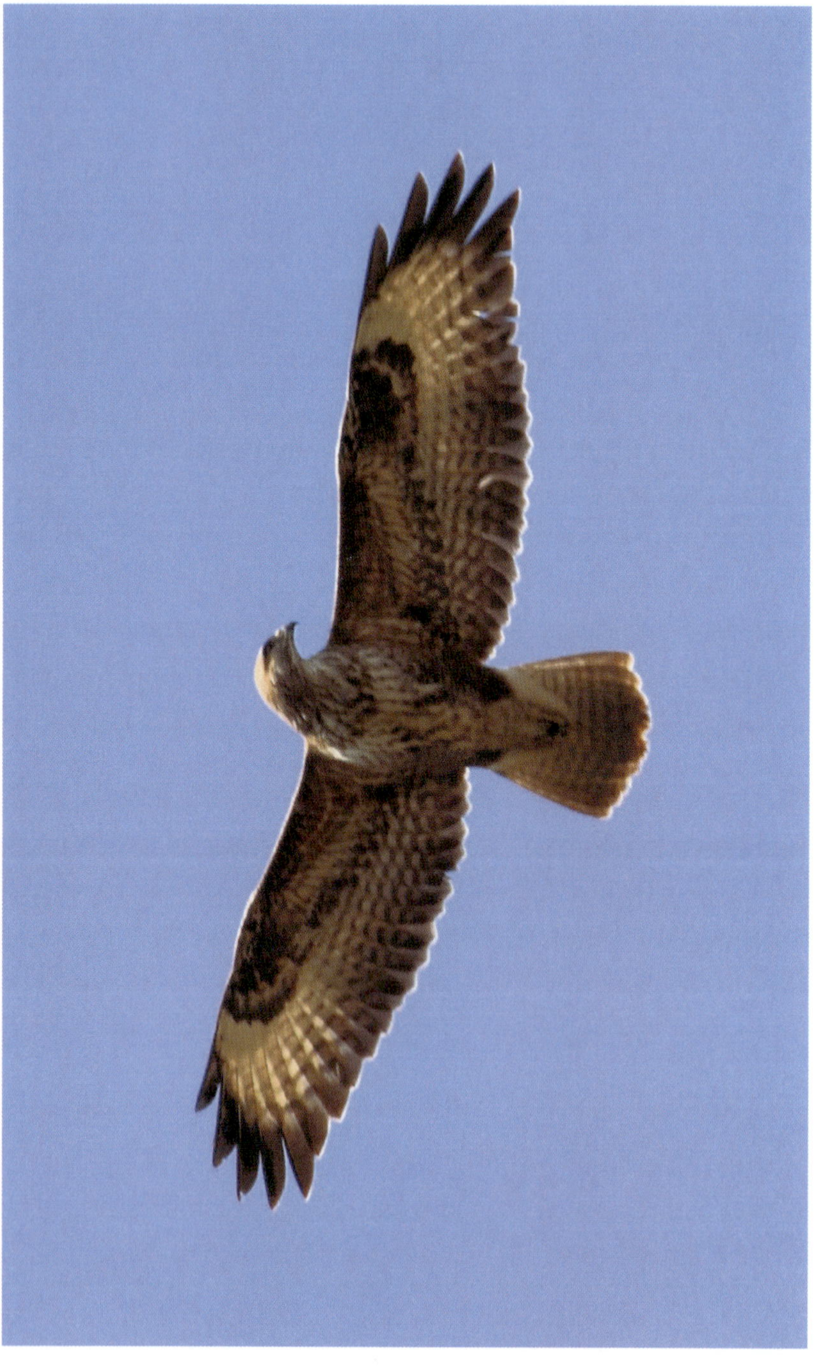

LIFE STAGES

The fact that Common Buzzards mate for life is well-known. When males desire to mate, they make a spectacular gesture to woo their female counterparts. They perform an aerial show dubbed *"the roller coaster."*

The bird's breeding season varies depending on where it lives. The season usually begins in March and ends in April. Female buzzards lay eggs at irregular intervals during the breeding season. Between two and six clutches are typical.

After a month and a week of incubation, the eggs hatch within a week. Females tend to stay in the nest to defend their young, while males hunt for food for the family. Young common buzzards leave the nest at the age of 14-16 weeks.

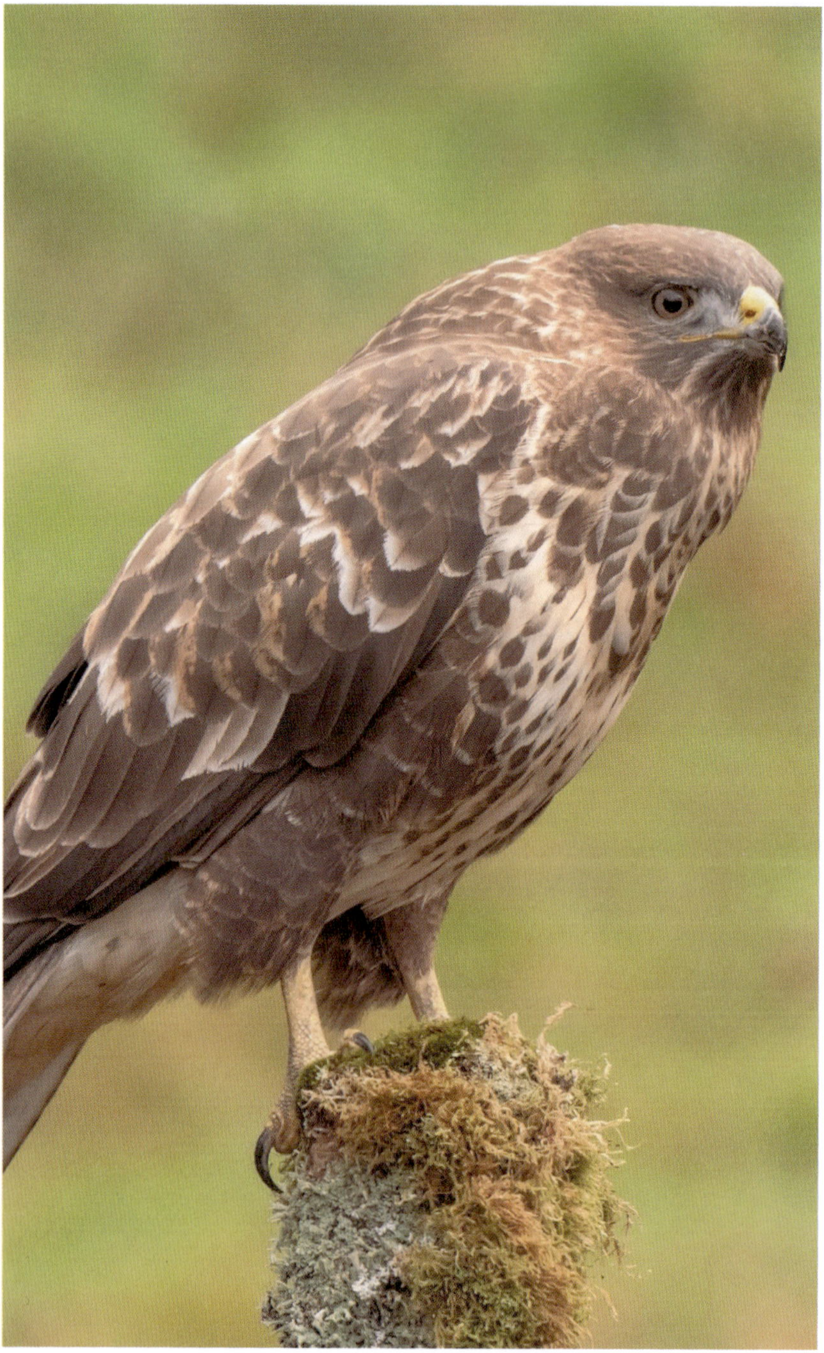

LIFE SPAN

The lifespan of the common buzzard is eight years on average. The destruction of nests and dangers from predators cause many of these birds to die young.

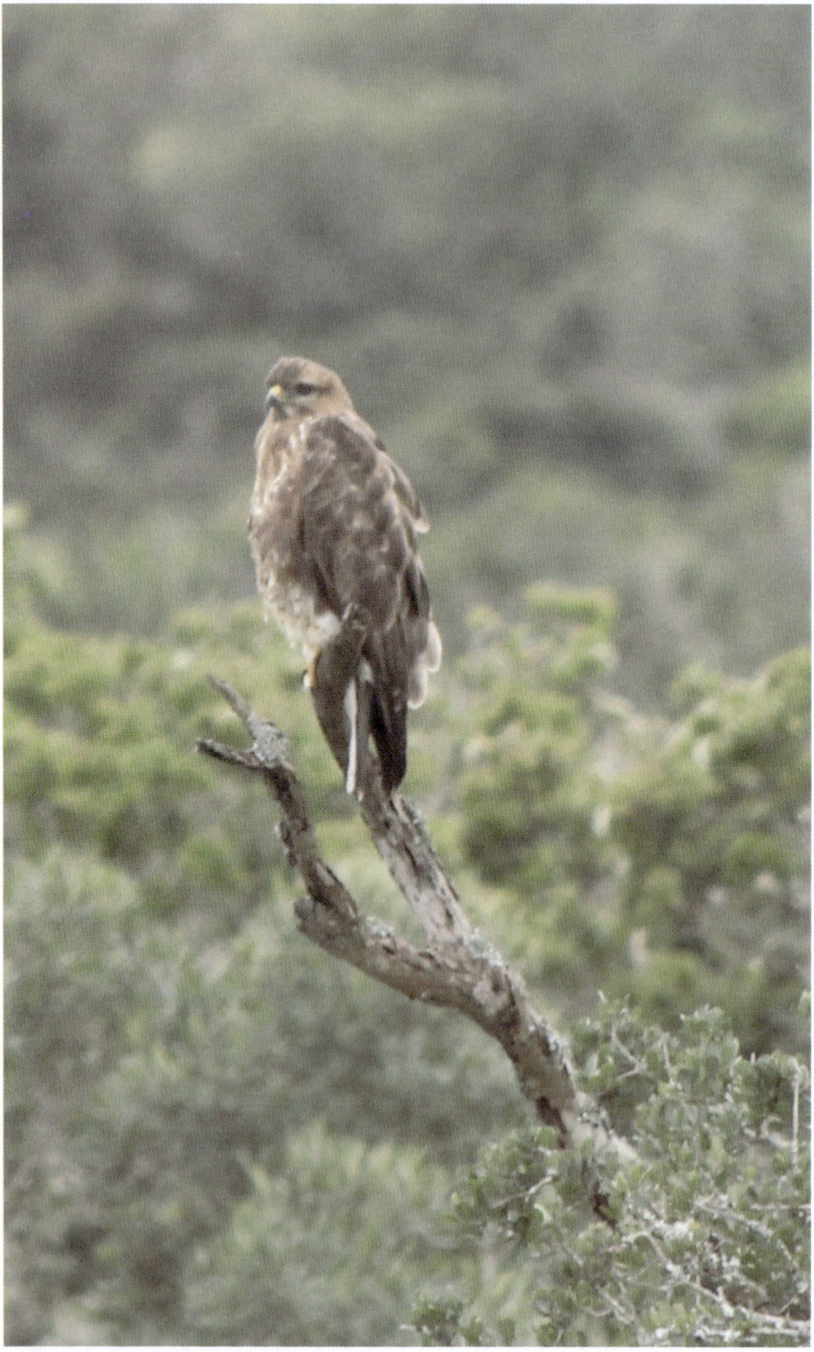

SIZE

Buzzards range in length from 15 to 23 inches. The Common Buzzard is a medium-sized bird with a wingspan of 43 to 49 inches. In this species of bird of prey, females are usually slightly larger than males.

Buzzards weigh between 1 and 3 pounds on average. Males of this species are noticeably lighter than females, allowing them to fly further and quicker within their range.

Buzzards may reach speeds of up to 28 miles per hour when in flight. Because of their wide and large wings, they can fly at very fast!

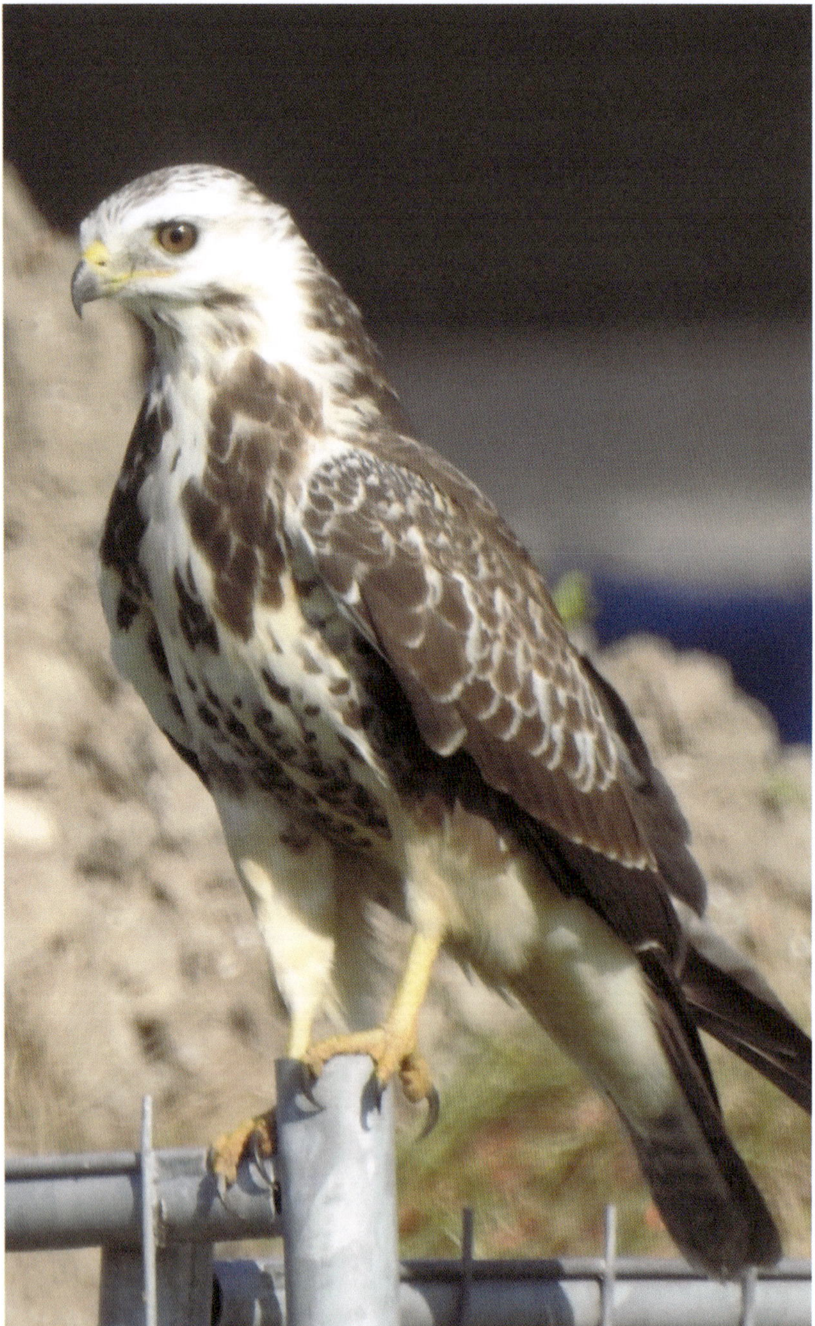

HABITAT

Buzzards are most typically found in Europe. This bird population is frequently seen in countries including the United Kingdom, France, and Greece.

In Asia, they can be found in India, Mongolia, and China. During the winter, the population has been known to move to African countries. Buzzards are commonly seen in rural areas, farmlands, and wooded areas. They prefer to live in open areas or near woodland edges. They are occasionally observed in wetlands and steep terrain.

With logs, branches, and twigs, these buzzards create a thick, hefty nest. To line the inside of the nest, these birds utilize heather or leaves. Many nests are made near the trunk of the tree or in a strong branch fork.

They can range in height from ten to eighty feet. On rocky cliffs, other Common Buzzards make their nests. Because these birds use the same nest year after year, the nest's size and shape may change as a result of maintenance efforts.

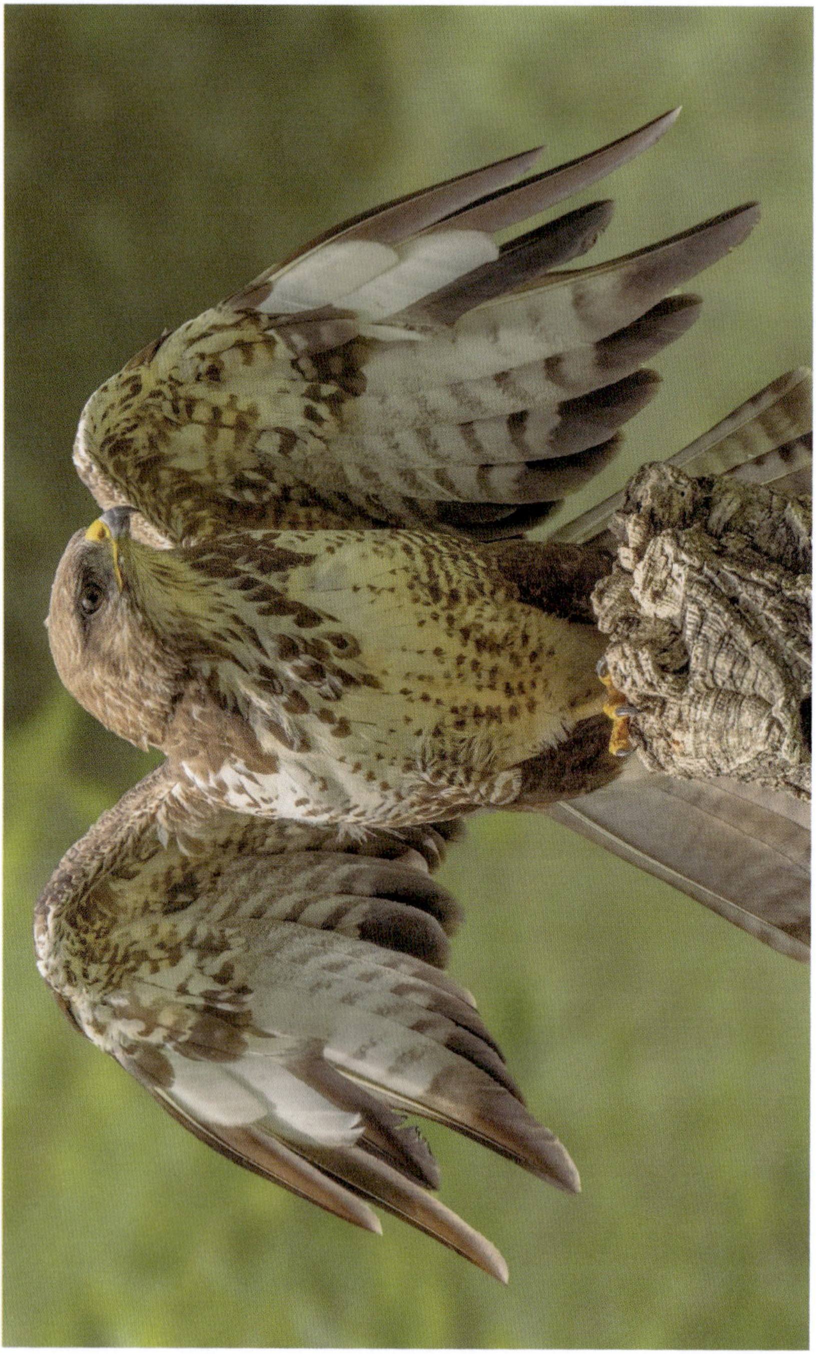

DIET

Buzzards are carnivorous birds that eat insects and small mammals. Their primary prey is rabbits, but they also eat rats, reptiles, and other small invertebrates. These birds stomp their feet on the ground to draw worms to the surface, where they can be eaten.

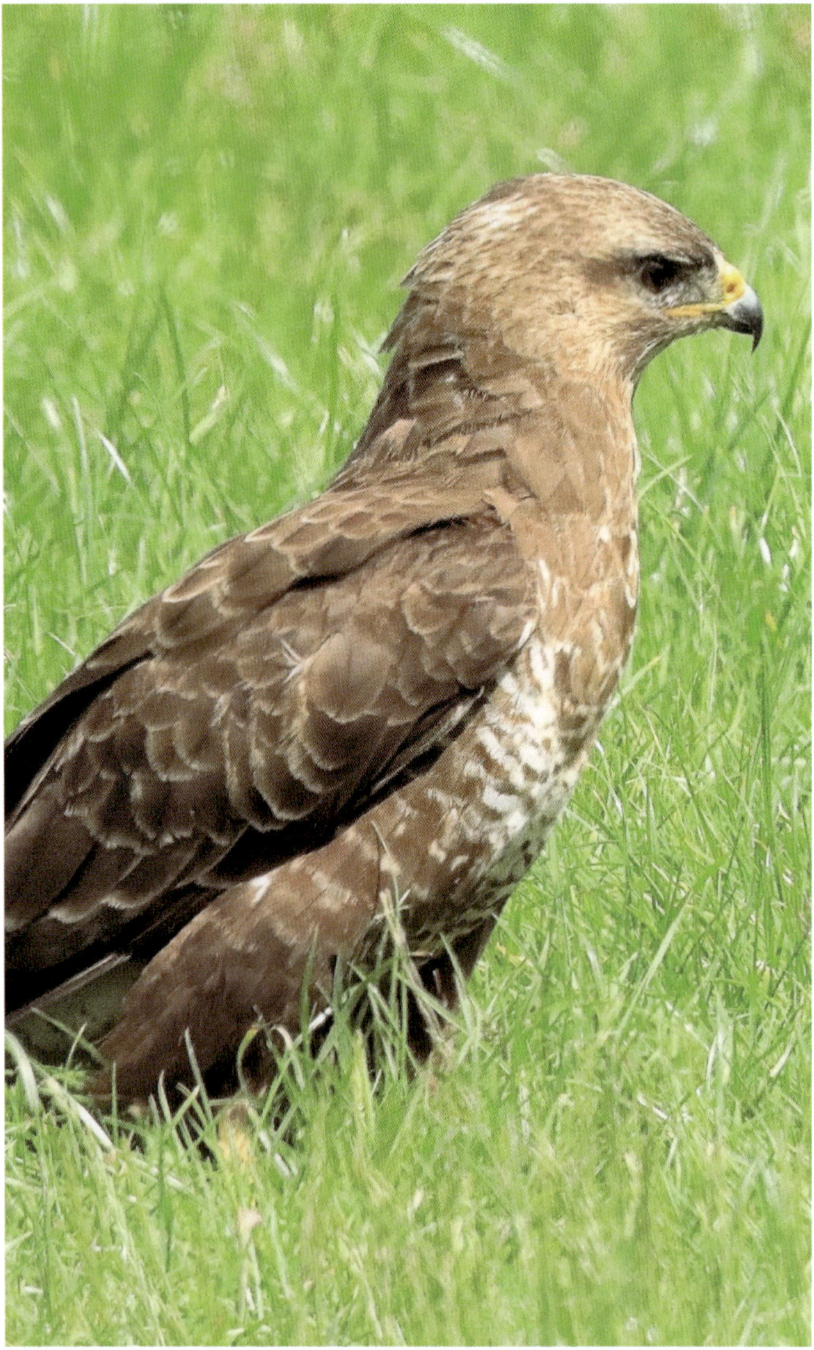

ENEMIES

Predators of this bird include eagles, wildcats, and foxes. Foxes and wildcats can sneak up on a bird as it eats carrion and captures it. These birds are smaller than eagles and can be overpowered by them.

These birds are also vulnerable to humans. People would sometimes lay out poisoned traps in order to get rid of a fox in the neighborhood, but this could be eaten by buzzards.

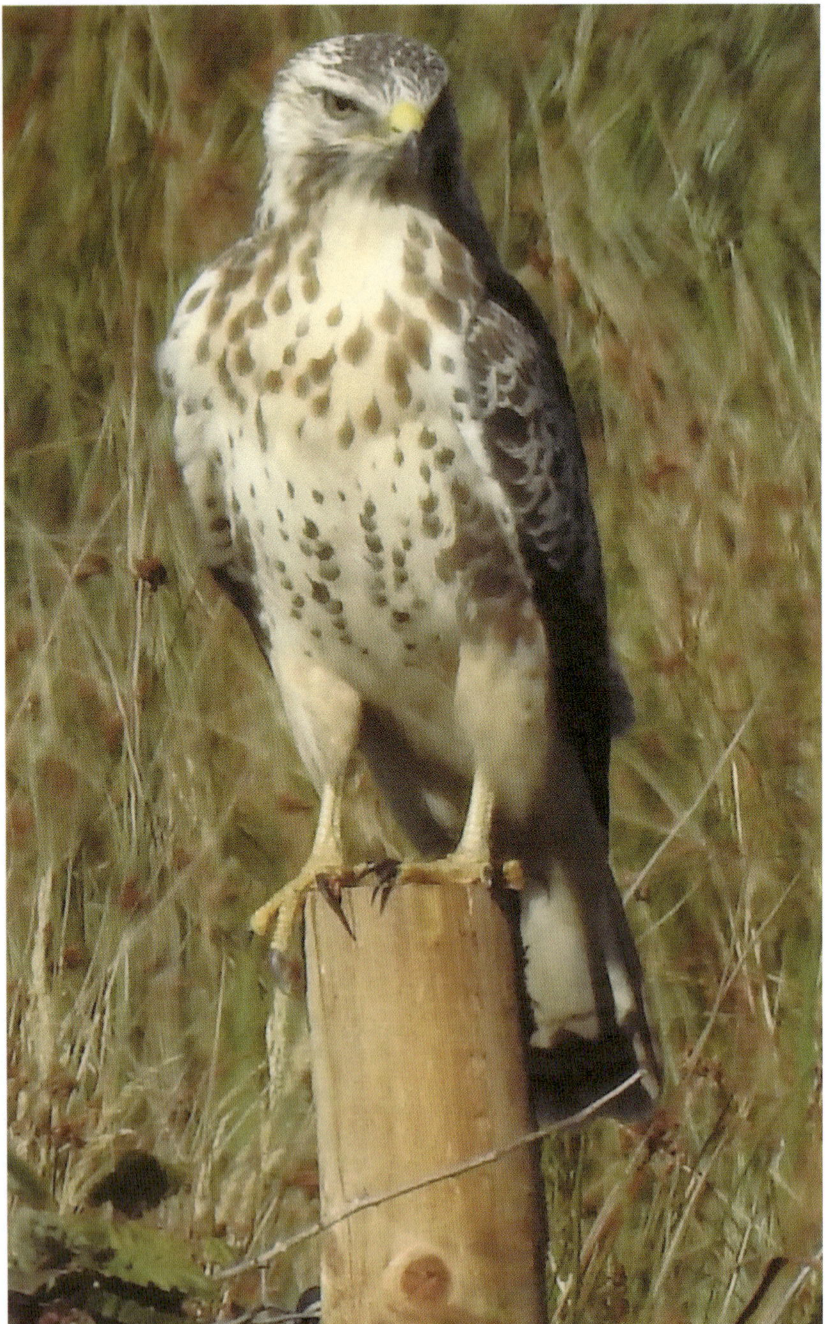

SUITABILITY AS PETS

In a nutshell, you cannot keep a Buzzard as a pet. You can, however, interact with them up close in a variety of ways. Visit a nearby wildlife center or zoo that has a buzzards living in an appropriate habitat there.

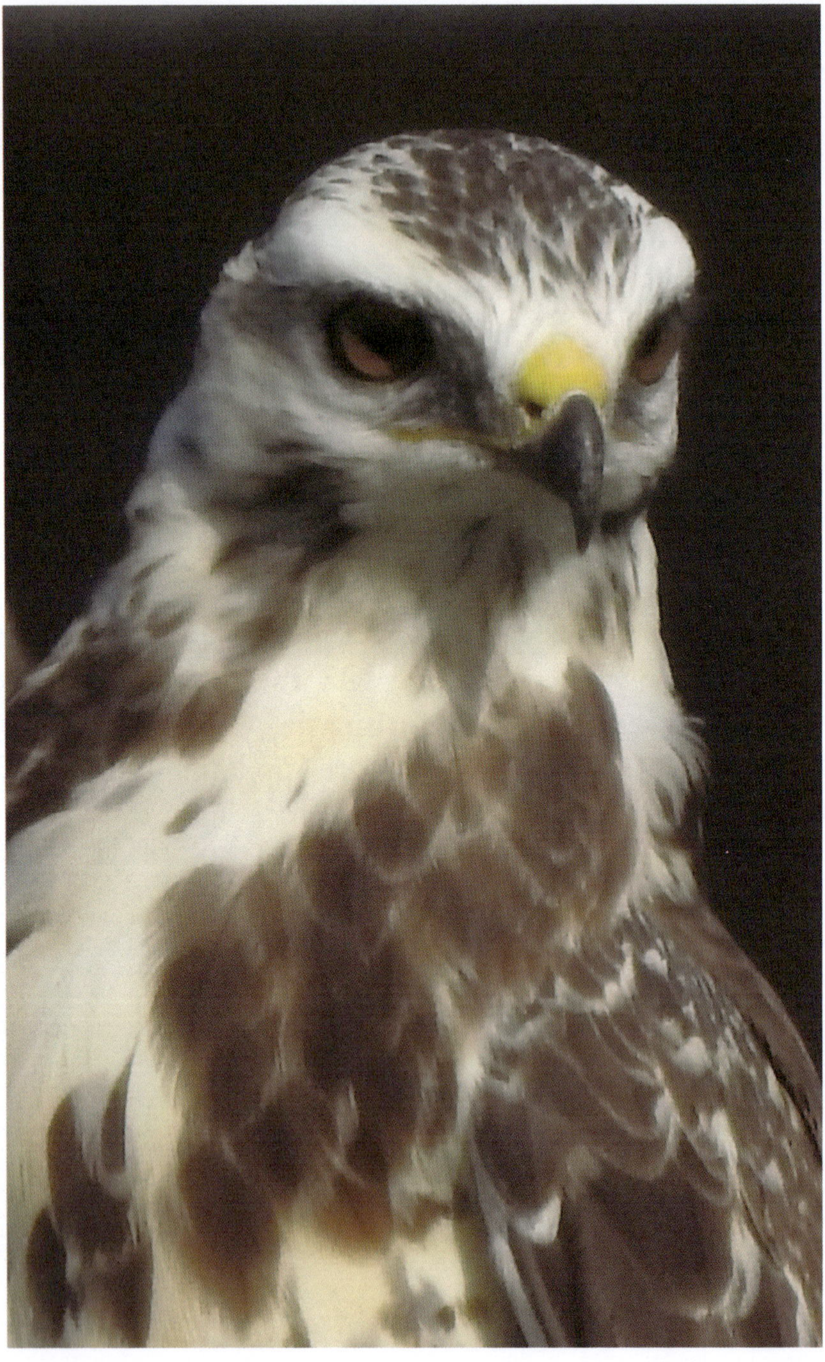

COLOR ME

COLOR ME

COLOR ME

COLOR ME

COLOR ME

COLOR ME

COLOR ME

COLOR ME

COLOR ME

COLOR ME

Please leave me a review here:

LisaStrattin.com/Review-Vol-506

For more Kindle Downloads Visit Lisa Strattin Author Page on Amazon Author Central

amazon.com/author/lisastrattin

To see upcoming titles, visit my website at LisaStrattin.com– most books available on Kindle!

LisaStrattin.com

FREE BOOK

FOR ALL SUBSCRIBERS – SIGN UP NOW

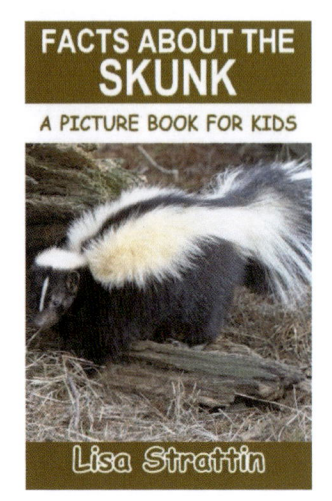

LisaStrattin.com/Subscribe-Here

LisaStrattin.com/Facebook

LisaStrattin.com/Youtube

Printed in Great Britain
by Amazon